A NEW ORDER

Apostolic & Prophetic Restoration of His Church

Daniel J. Richardson

A New Order:
Apostolic & Prophetic Restoration of His Church

Copyright © 2017 Daniel J. Richardson

All rights reserved. Printed in the United States of America. No part of this book may be used or reproduced in any manner whatsoever without written permission except in the case of brief quotations in critical articles or reviews.

Unless otherwise noted, all Bible quotations are from the New King James Version of the Bible.

Cover Design: SLE Designz
Typesetting, Book Layout by Enger Lanier Taylor of In Due Season Publishing

Published By: In Due Season Publishing
                Huntsville, Alabama
                indueseasonpublishing@gmail.com
                www.indueseasonpublishing.com

ISBN-13: 978-0972745697
ISBN-10: 0972745696

To order additional copies, please contact

Bishop Daniel Richardson
6831 Hollow Road | Huntsville, AL 35810
Phone: 256.851.1788
www.e-nest.org

First and foremost, I thank the Lord for the great and wonderful things He continues to do in my life. To Him be all glory and honor for the blessed revelation and understanding of HIS Word.

Bishop Daniel J. Richardson

Dedication

In loving memory of my parents, the late Garnell and Essie Richardson. Special thanks to my wife, Tiffany; children, Daniel, Joshua, Christian, Jasmine and Gabriel. The tremendous support from my siblings, my Eagles' Nest Ministries Church and the many wonderful spiritual sons and daughters that encouraged me to do this, especially Elders Stanley and Tonya Parker, Elder Calvin and Brit Mitchell. Finally, thank the Lord for the great things He continues to do in my life.

Bishop Donald Hilliard, Jr., D. Min
The Cathedral International, Senior Pastor
Perth Amboy, NJ

The Scripture says, "Surely the Lord God does nothing, unless He reveals His secrets to His servants the Prophets" (Amos 3:7). Bishop Daniel J. Richardson is one that has a credible Apostolic and Prophetic voice; as such these teachings will help expand what we are doing. We undergird it, we affirm the work of The Lord, and we affirm him as an Apostle and a Prophet in this hour. We agree with the call of God on his life, and we thank God for this available vessel that has dedicated his life for Kingdom purposes.

Bishop H. Curtis Douglas, **Senior Pastor**
Dabar Bethlehem Cathedral
Presiding Prelate of Covenant Fellowship Alliance
Queens Village, New York

From the inception of the Church, God has appointed certain people to be leaders in the movement. In the listing of the five-fold ministry gifts, the first two mentioned are the Apostle and Prophet. The first supplies governmental leadership, while the other gives direction obtained from The Lord. Eagles' Nest Ministries Church is blessed to have a man that flows in both of those giftings (as well as many others in the five-fold list). Bishop Daniel J. Richardson is a leader with an Apostolic/Prophetic call on his life. His works speak for him. They show that he is gifted in both the governing and guiding of God's Kingdom in this 21st century.

Pastor Tyrone (TY) & Lady Shirelle Bennett
Ekklesia Kingdom Ministries
Bel Air, MD

As a GIFT given to the Body of Christ, Bishop Daniel J. Richardson has committed his life to the call and the cause of the Kingdom! He is a powerful orator of the Word and one who releases the voice of God with Prophetic precision. Bishop Richardson is a man "set and sent" by God to bring revelation and truth to the times in which we live and we are eternally grateful for his Apostolic imprint upon our lives and ministry!

Elder Calvin Mitchell
Eagles' Nest Director of Strategic Planning/Policies
President/CEO Sarai Services Group, Inc.
Huntsville, AL

Bishop Daniel Richardson delivers a very powerful confirmation of God's Prophetic order and His call for us to demonstrate His Apostolic and Prophetic mandate in the earth. Our talents are His resources for Kingdom building, maturing of the Saints and manifestation of His promises for us. This book is a precise account, a demonstration and explanation of God's expectation of our walk *with* and *for* Him, as well as His expectation of our execution of His Apostolic will.

Minister Nicholas Bhones
Son, Eagles' Nest Ministries Church
Huntsville, AL

When it comes to the Apostle and the Prophet, both are crucial in laying the foundation and the building of a local Church, a network of Churches, as well as the establishment of foreign Churches abroad. The Apostle is needed for breaking and establishing new ground, new dimensions in God and providing strategy of purpose and order within enemy lines. Prophets bring the HEAT, the fire, the passion, and a sense of NOW/URGENCY to God's people and God's House.

I would like to equate it to a ship's captain who cannot sail alone; he must have assistance and/or crew to maintain the ship on its preordained course to its final destination. Similarly, the Apostle needs the Prophet to assist in navigating new territories and new lands for Kingdom building. At no time is this saying that the Apostle isn't Prophetic, because he/she truly must be acutely attuned to God's timing. They must be deliberately susceptible to God's strategic maneuverability and placements in order to be victorious while on missions always mindful that spiritual warfare yields profound Prophetic ability with the Prophet. God has called the Apostle and Prophet to work together; managing and developing an administration of leadership within a person or established Churches established by the Apostle. However, the Prophet while working with the Apostle is more driven toward the renewal and continued movements forward. They are constantly pushing towards hitting the mark of destiny and purpose. Apostles and Prophets are not only builders, but they bless the Body of Christ. While the enemy attempted to divide the Apostle and Prophet, you will see through this book how God has always desired that they work together to cause a mighty, continual blow to the enemy of our soul!! Allow this book to position you for your place in the Kingdom and watch your life shift like never before.

Prophetess Tonya Parker
Trailblazers International Ministries
Huntsville, AL

If you know me, then you know that I am all about a person reaching their full potential by fulfilling their purpose and destiny in God. As I think back over my life, I realize that the hand of an Apostle or Prophet has been used to facilitate every turn, shift, push, and pull into my destiny. God uses Apostles and Prophets to introduce and activate His people into fresh new dimensions in Him. As a body of believers who fulfill all that God desires and destined us to be, we must get back to the divine order of God. People of God, I admonish you to not only embrace the part of God that's comfortable for you, but perfect, and yes, operate in it as well. As a people, we are to embrace all that God is; which includes the five-fold ministry gifts of the Apostle, the Prophet, the Evangelist, the Pastor, and the Teacher. They were given to serve as gifts to us all. I don't know about you, but when I receive gifts, I'm not one to leave them wrapped up, but I can't wait to unwrap them, and see what's under the wrapping so that I can make good use of the gift that I have been given. There is no need to be afraid of God-given gifts. The enemy will always send forth counterfeits, but as it says in *Deuteronomy 11:32*....those that know their God will be strong and do exploits.

It is time that we get to know God in a greater way; and not be afraid to step out of our comfort zones. After all, there are people waiting on us to come forth and arrive at the place called purpose and destiny. God declares to you today that NOW; RIGHT NOW is the time for you to ARISE and SHINE, for your light has come. For the glory of the Lord will rise upon you. Why? Because the Lord Himself, has need of you.

Biography

Go through, go through the gates; prepare ye the way of the people; cast up, cast up the highway; gather out the stones; lift up a standard for the people.
Isaiah 62:10

Bishop Daniel J. Richardson is an Apostolic Prophetic Visionary who thirsts after the heart of God. He currently serves as the Senior Pastor of Eagles' Nest Ministries Church (ENMC) in Huntsville, Alabama. As a spiritual "tent-maker," Bishop Richardson exercises his God-given, Kingdom authority to minister to the masses, discipleship and evangelism. He is committed to equipping the saints of Eagles' Nest and the surrounding community for the work of ministry while teaching excellence in execution in every facet of ministry. Under his hand, ENMC has been forging new ground as an Apostolic Prophetic Church with over 35 functional ministries, fully operational in Five-Fold Ministry for the purpose of remapping the spiritual landscape of the region, over which God has given him oversight.

On December 1, 2012, Bishop Richardson was Consecrated a Prince in the Lord's Church by his Apostolic Father in the Faith, Bishop Donald Hilliard, II, Senior Pastor Cathedral International (Perth Amboy, NJ) and Presiding Prelate Emeritus of the Covenant Ecumenical Fellowship and Cathedral Assemblies (CEFCA). Bishop Hilliard was joined by Co-Consecrators, Bishop H. Curtis Douglas and Bishop L. Spenser Smith, Episcopates from both the Joint College of African American Pentecostal Bishops, where the Archbishop J. Delano Ellis, II, serves as Metropolitan-Archbishop, and Kingdom Fellowship College of Bishops, where Bishop Ralph Dennis is the Presiding Prelate, respectively. It was during this process that Bishop Richardson was formally inducted as a Joint College Episcopate.

Bishop Richardson is also the visionary and chief executive officer of DJR Gateway To The Nations Covenant Ministries (DJR GTTN)—his personal ministry, birthed by the Holy Spirit, to expand his spiritual "sphere of influence" from a local pastorate to one that would anticipate and then meet the needs of pastors, Churches and ministries in a regional, national, and international realm. He is established in covenant relationship while providing spiritual guidance and covering to pastors, Churches, para-Ministries and businesses. Through these connections, his international ministry has reached mission fields in Egypt, Germany, Mozambique, Japan, Afghanistan, Asia, Korea, Columbia, Philippines and Israel.

Bishop Daniel Richardson is a graduate of the University of Alabama, School of Engineering. He is the son of the late Deacon Garnell and Mother Essie Richardson of Shady Grove, Alabama. He is married to the lovely Lady Tiffany Elizabeth and he is the proud father of five wonderful children: Daniel, Joshua, Christian, Jasmine and Gabriel Timothy.

By the unction of the Holy Spirit, this "champion of change" is a chosen vessel of God, who is fully committed to the cause of Christ...and doing all to the glory of Almighty God.

A New Order

Apostolic & Prophetic Restoration of His Church

And are built upon the foundation of the Apostles and Prophets, Jesus Christ himself being the chief corner stone; In whom all the building fitly framed together groweth unto an holy temple in the Lord: In whom ye also are builded together for an habitation of God through the Spirit.
Ephesians 2:20-22

Everything that God does is with a plan and a purpose in mind. Building Him an Apostolic and Prophetic House means that you must become an architect; a master builder in the hands of God, who is the greatest Master Architect of all time; erecting His Temple, His House, His Church in the earth. Growing up, we were always taught that the Church is the pillar of every community. Well, that still holds true today; and Jesus Christ is the Cornerstone of the Church. It is His house and He uses His gifts, to include the Apostles and Prophets to ensure that the foundation is not just laid, but that it's laid according to the blueprint of heaven. Here we see the Apostle Paul specifically identifying the Apostle and the Prophet as the ones that would build upon the foundation that Christ laid to shift the paradigm of the Kingdom of God back to mankind. As we know, it was in the Garden of Eden that man lost his authority to walk in dominion in the earth realm. At Calvary, Christ became the panacea, the solution, to restore back that authority and dominion.

The Building Blueprint

In *Ezekiel 40-48*, God gives specific instructions of what He desires His house to look like. It's no different today. Every part of the blueprint of God's House has a specific design, measurement, and purpose for Kingdom advancement. Although we know that God chose David to be king to the children of Israel, it was in 1 Chronicles that David began to address the fact that he was chosen to lead the people, but it would be Solomon that actually built the Lord's House. Solomon, in fact, built upon the foundation of his father David, whereas, the succession, the legacy and the heritage of the kingdom would continue. Hence, the Apostolic and Prophetic giftings are set to build upon the foundation that Christ set in reestablishing the Kingdom of God in the earth realm to operate and function in dominion.

Peter continues this thinking as he describes it in 1 Peter 2:5. It is in this regard that the Lord's intention is to establish a kingdom that will serve not as a stumbling block, but rather as a building block that will create a culture of spiritual authority and power.

> *Ye also, as lively stones, are built up a spiritual house, an holy priesthood, to offer up spiritual sacrifices, acceptable to God by Jesus Christ. Wherefore also it is contained in the scripture, Behold, I lay in Sion a chief corner stone, elect, precious: and he that believeth on him shall not be confounded. Unto you therefore which believe he is precious: but unto them which be disobedient, the stone which the builders disallowed, the same is made the head of the corner, And a stone of stumbling, and a rock of offence, even to them which stumble at the word, being disobedient: whereunto also they were appointed. 1Peter 2:5-8*

When it comes to building God a House, one thing is for certain, Jesus must be the foundation. Without Him, there is no House! Now, I know many are saying, "But wait, that's not what He told Peter in Matthew 16:18, when He said that upon this rock He would build His Church." The rock that Jesus is talking about is the revelation that Peter gave regarding Jesus being the Christ, the Son of the Living God. This revelation allows individuals the opportunity to build an Apostolic culture that cannot be penetrated by forces of evil. In fact, that house is built on a solid foundation and what the Apostle and Prophet does is advance and strengthen the Believers further with greater spiritual insight. I agree, the Church, The Body is built on the principles, the strength, and the ability to win souls. However, every structure must have a solid foundation or it will not last, and that foundation is Jesus Christ. What we must understand is that what is even greater than the building that is erected is the foundation that it stands upon. To truly understand the importance of the cornerstone, just talk with any Master Builder. I am sure they will tell you that when erecting any type of building or structure, the cornerstone is the most important part of the structure! It is, indeed, the foundational crux, the keystone for whatever is being built – all else depends on the cornerstone as the core point of measure. The cornerstone is the connecting force of two particular things. It is Christ the Cornerstone who connects the gifts and Body for the purpose of Kingdom advancement. The cornerstone is what will determine the height, the depth, the width, the total circumference and the linchpin of stability of the structure that will be erected. God always had a desire to use the Apostles and Prophets to ensure that the structure, the order of God, was properly laid at the very foundation. However, He will not do that until we take our rightful place.

It was the very genius of God that He used a member of the Godhead (His Son) to restore the broken relationship. In Ephesians 2:18, the text says that it was through Christ we have access back to the Father. Christ was part of the plan to RECONNECT us back to the Father. Therefore, by Christ, our dominion has been restored and our relationship has been reconnected back to God, the Father, through the Holy Spirit. Once the reconnection and restoration occurred, Christ then used key representatives in the Kingdom of God to reflect the paradigm shift and expand it to the point that its influence rejected the objective of the kingdom of darkness, which is to steal, kill and destroy. Those representatives (once trained and true to the call), then picked up the mantle of Christ and began to demonstrate His power in the earth realm. Hence, the Apostles and Prophets serve as key mantle pieces to display and deliver the agenda of the Kingdom of God. They bring Apostolic governmental order to those that are willing to receive a new dimension of power and authority. They are able to establish a new order in the earth realm on behalf of the Kingdom. Prophetically, they speak truth to power so that the very person of Christ is emulated and replicated to be as He is in the world. In fact, when people see the functioning of the office, there ought to be a reflection of Christ so powerfully displayed that His glory is seen.

This is the case when Peter moved about and His shadow impacted those that encountered it. The same is true for Paul, whose handkerchiefs and aprons were used for healing and deliverance. Indeed this same power and demonstration is necessary to build the confidence and faith of the people to once again dominate in the earth realm as sons of God. All of this establishes a dwelling place for God in the earth! *Ephesians 2:22* says, *"We are built together for a habitation of God through the Spirit."* The ultimate rationale for a continuation of this shift is that there would be a continuous place for God to live in the earth.

As with anything that has human hands and intellect involved, one can look up at any given moment and realize that the Temple; the house, is not according to the original blueprint of God. When that realization occurs, one must not be too prideful nor afraid to start over again. Starting over again is not a bad thing; especially if the end result is what God had in mind from the beginning of time. When we realize that we must start again, we must become spiritual master builders and begin to excavate the current ground that we have found ourselves standing on. To excavate is to make a hole or a channel by digging; to remove earth, or ground, carefully and systematically from a particular area. We find in *Jeremiah 1:10* that God told Jeremiah, *"See, I have this day set thee over the nations and over the kingdoms, to root out, and to pull down, and to destroy, and to throw down, to build, and to plant."*

Apostles and Prophets are the master builders in the earth. This does not mean that the rest of the body is not needed but it does mean that until the Apostle and Prophet come together the House cannot be built according to the plans of heaven. To fully understand the pattern, we simply must begin to understand the role and function of the Apostle and Prophet. These two offices were designed to work together to bring forth the plans and purposes of God in the earth.

Every Apostle is a master builder sent by God. The key word here is *sent*. You cannot rightfully be an Apostle and not go anywhere. Apostles are territory-takers for the Kingdom of God. As Apostles, our assignment is to bring order in the earth and to disrupt systems of darkness. Our role in the earth is to provide direction, input, and guidance when there is none. Apostles carry a fathering anointing. Instead of being consumed with erecting buildings, our primary focus is to build the people for the glory of God.

As Apostles and Prophets, we have been given the daunting task of working hand in hand while leading the way and building on the foundation of Jesus Christ. Everything that God does is already finished. When He shows us our assignment, He reveals it to us in its completed state, because it is already finished! As Apostles and Prophets join together for kingdom advancement, there will be a Spirit of Truth that is released. When truth is released, there is a shifting that will take place in the hearts and minds of those that this truth is imparted. Once you come into the knowledge of truth, there's no way that you can "unknow" what you have been exposed to! I absolutely love exposure. It is a key ingredient when it comes to forging ahead into the greater works of Christ. In fact, exposure is a precursor to expansion. The Lord desires that we not just know a thing, but that revelation encompasses what we know. Knowledge without revelation is simply information. The Lord desires that we not just know a thing, but we become so empowered by the revelation that we actually employ the thing as an advantage in Kingdom Building.

Apostolic and Prophetic Advancement

For far too long there has been no true Apostolic and Prophetic activity in the earth;

1 Samuel 3:1 is a depiction of a time when there was no Apostolic movement or any Prophetic activity. During this time the Prophet Samuel began to develop a Prophetic ministry, along with a company of Prophets. It is the heart of God to release that same type of ministry today. Samuel was a typology of a spiritual father or an Apostle during that time. God has called Apostles to raise up and train young emerging Prophets so that they may eventually walk hand in hand to help transition the body of Christ to the next dimension in the earth. By the time the scriptures get to 1 Samuel 19, Samuel has raised up an entire company of Prophets. Apostles are called to train, activate, and release. All of us are unique with our own gifts and callings. At our core, Apostles and Prophets are the same all over the world. It is time that we begin to execute the universal mission just as God ordained and Christ commissioned. God is calling for His Church to raise up a banner, to become a visibly elevated standard so that His body can see the Church moving and marching forward.

God wants to increase the Prophetic in His house. It is His desire to send a wave of His glory in His house that can only come by way of the Prophetic. The Prophet is needed in the Church today, because it is the Prophet that will see first when the Church is misaligned. God has designed and built the Prophet in such a way to help ensure that the Church stays on course. As Apostles called by God, the ministry gift of the Prophet should not be feared but must be embraced. Their role in the body should not be rejected, but we must learn to receive them with open arms. As we look within many Churches today, we can all agree that we need the ministry of the Prophet to see exactly what we are or are not doing, what needs to shift, and how much of it needs to be changed. God has called His Prophet to be the one that "sees," but has oftentimes been ignored. It is time that we, as Apostolic fathers, begin to restore the Prophet and allow them to be all that God has commanded them to be so they can begin to remove all blind spots out of His Church.

I believe that at the end of the day the world is trying to catch up Prophetically to what the Lord has already released or has already done in the earth realm. The release is imminent and now we must catch and covey what He has done. It is time that we understand and receive the creativity of God, as it relates to everything that He has given us as His children. At the end of the day, my assignment is to help you be all that you can be in God, so that ultimately God can be all that He needs to be in your life. It is in this season that He is releasing a fresh supply of revelation and vision, and He is doing it by way of His Apostles and Prophets. Whenever you hear the truth being released through the word of God, there must be a response. In this season, God is charging the Apostle and the Prophet to pave the way, train others to receive the Word of the Lord, and then open their mouths and deliver that which He is saying to His Church.

As carriers of His Glory, we are called to not only house His glory, but to release it in the earth. We have literally entered into our Apostolic Prophetic defining moment. As a believer, you must grab hold to the horns of the altar and do not let them go until everything you are believing God for has come to pass. The faith to believe at that level is a faith that has been imparted through generations. There are promises that God has in store for your life. Do not let them go until you see them manifest. Do not let go until all that He has promised has broken through every opposing force. It is time for the Body of Christ to arise and walk in the promised peace of God, which passes all natural understanding and releases joy that is overflowing.

The Assignment

In *Ephesians 4*, Paul reminds us that Apostles, Prophets, Evangelists, Pastors and Teachers, were left as Christ's representatives in the earth, and their assignment specifically is to advance the Kingdom of God in the earth. In order to do this, the Apostle and the Prophet are needed to forge the way. We must decipher how this would look. When all of the gifts come together collectively, these representatives will be regarded as gifts from Christ. He gave these royal representatives to help mature the saints. Maturing of the saints requires that we grow up in God to the point that we are no longer operating and functioning in a place of defeat. From this place we recognize that we can eat. Not only are we able to partake of milk, but we have the propensity to chew on the meat of the Word of God and digest it. We must have strong meat in order to fully survive life's greatest challenges.

These gifts are employed to assist the saints in the work of the ministry. Notice He did not say working in ministry, but *the work* of the ministry. The work of the ministry is not just that which is confined to the local Church ministry. It is a lifestyle that conveys the effectiveness of the impact of the assignment. The work of the ministry is the empowering, enlightening, embracing and establishment of people that reflect God in the earth realm. The work of the ministry is teaching all nations, baptizing them in the Holy Ghost and bringing about a spiritual awakening to represent the very essence of God.

These gifts or representatives are commissioned to edify the Body of Christ. Simply, this means that they are to build people up. Certainly, we do not have to look far to see that people need to be built up. In a world where the enemy is insistent on destroying and tearing down the lives of

God's people, the assignment of these representatives is to build up, encourage and strengthen those that are in the Body of Christ. We must begin to convey that even when we are weak, in our physical bodies, we are indeed <u>strong</u> in God spiritually.

Gifts are not all inclusive, but must bring about a unity of the faith. Unity of faith implies that we be united in what we believe; and that our faith is indeed strong. We cannot be an Apostolic Prophetic people and be weak in our faith. Indeed, our faith allows us to move mountains, walk on water, open blind eyes, heal sick bodies, raise the dead, shake off venomous snakes and simply lead the unredeemed to Christ. It is time that we begin to speak those things that be not, as though they were. Regardless of any current situations that we may face, our Prophetic precision should cause us to speak heaven into earth with accuracy.

The Apostle and Prophet are NECESSARY in this 21st Century now more than ever. As saints of God, we need to see Him operating in our lives with demonstration and power. Our current world system needs a divine makeover. It is in this hour through the ministry of the Apostle and Prophet that nations will be turned upside down. This will not be done without opposition, but we all know that the enemy's opposition becomes our opportunity and confirmation, that we are indeed headed in the right direction.

In the book of Nehemiah, when it was time to build the House of God, the Bible said, Nehemiah was being challenged by people all around him. They were challenging his purpose and his instruction to build again. You see, when you are trying to build anything for the Kingdom of God you will be opposed by the enemy. Every effort will be made to cause heartache, strife and distractions. This is why it is imperative that you know what kind of work you are doing. If you do not know your assignment in the earth, life's challenges just might cause you to come down, and quit in the process. As for me, I have come too far to turn back now, and the Lord has given me too much to let go.

There are people that might walk away. However, you have got to learn to be ok with that. Give the peace sign and let them go on and do what they are going to do. Prophetically, I tell you today that this is the season that God will take you from glory to glory. It will start with you making a declaration out of your own mouth that, "If you are going to leave me, you should have left me before now." This is the time that God has revealed His hands on my life and I believe that it is important that you connect yourself with the right people. If you are not connected with the right people, then it's time to let some people go. If they are not helping you advance and pushing you forward to do greater works, then it's time to say goodbye.

The Set

The Bible says in *1Corinthians 12:28*, *"And God hath set some in the Church, first apostles, secondarily prophets, thirdly teachers, after that miracles, then gifts of healings, helps, governments, diversities of tongues."* There are some things that God has set in place. God said it and you cannot unsay it. God has set some Apostles. You must understand the anointing and the assignment of the Apostle is to set governmental order, and to fully establish the Church. That is what Paul was doing as he went through his missionary journeys. He would be sent by God, to go and establish Churches and Kingdom order in those Churches.

The Bible says specifically that God set first the Apostles. This is the order of God, so the Apostolic anointing might Prophetically move in an atmosphere and release heaven on earth. This says that even in a place where we find ourselves struggling and we show up in an atmosphere that has been set by God, the Apostolic anointing is sent there to break off certain things. An Apostolic, Prophetic house is a house of deliverance; a house whose assignment is to deliver us from proclivities, issues and problems that would prohibit us from being everything that we are supposed to be in God. The Apostles are certainly responsible for establishing Apostolic governmental order for the Church.

There are two forms of Holy inspired speech that is specifically mentioned when it comes to the Prophetic. The Nabi and the Roeh, or the Seer; the Nabi means an uttering forth as water springing forth out of a fountain. It is the word of God that is in you that begins to prophesy the very heartbeat of God. The spoken word that is coming forth is what causes lives to be changed and people to be set free. When you are a Nabi Prophet, there is an unctioning that comes upon you as the Spirit of God bubbles up on the inside of you. That is when you will speak His oracles, mysteries, wisdom, clarity, ways, and direction.

Then there is the Roeh or a Seer. The Seer sees visions; that is how Prophetic revelation is communicated to God's Prophet. The Seer is one that has the ability to see, has the ability to go behind the door of the Spirit realm; and see the things of God. The Seer is one who operates behind the scenes. God allows them to not just have outsight but insight. They are able to see things that are not shown in the natural necessarily, but in the Spirit.

Both the Nabi and the Seer are needed in the Kingdom to assist the Apostle for Kingdom advancement; and they should be planted in all of God's Houses. Some people will flow as a Nabi, and others, as Seers. As an Apostolic and Prophetic people, we all have some degree of the Prophetic operating within us, simply because the Holy Spirit lives on the inside of each of us. The Holy Spirit is forever communicating, leading and guiding us into all truth. Christ left a diversity of anointings in the earth, which means that one does not have to be confined or limited to a particular expression. As an Apostolic and Prophetic people, though we all have the ability to prophesy (receive a divine message from God), the office of the Prophet stretches wider. Contrary to popular belief, Prophets do more than just prophesy. Those that walk hand in hand with the Apostle in the office of the Prophet know that their first call is one of intercession. They are prayer warriors who stand in the gap for the people of God. Prophets worship, teach Prophetic lessons, release Prophetic sermons, impart, ignite fresh fire, watch, guard, deliver, heal, rebuke, judge, identify gifts and callings and set individuals in those gifts and callings. They help people transition from one dimension to the next; they gauge timing, have dreams and visions and pull up what has managed to get in the soil of the Spirit. They also plow out, root out, tear down and bless the people of God.

Thirdly, the teacher is the one who labors in Word. The teacher ensures that the Apostles and Prophets don't go outside the Word of God. It is the teacher that labors in doctrine with or without a pastoral charge. The teacher serves in the local Church to help us understand or bring light to the Word of God. Teachers will validate the word that is released and make sure that it is scripturally sound. God is giving us revelation of His Word every day. He shines a spotlight on particular scriptures so that we can implement the revelation in our everyday life. Teachers will break down the word so that everyone is able to understand the scriptures better. After all, the ones that have been given the revelation are the ones that will be able to express it best. A teacher is one that God will call to take His Word and make it so plain and descriptive to you, that you will understand it at any level. This does not mean that they water the Word down for your understanding, but it does mean that they are operating so strongly in their gift that no matter what level of understanding you possess, you will comprehend exactly what the message is that the Lord is trying to convey to you. God has gifted the teacher in such a way that you will be able to not just eat what is being taught, but you will be able to digest the Word that you are hearing. *Habakkuk 2* says, 'write the vision, make it plain and those that read might be able to run with it.' When you have been taught the Word, you know the Word and the Word knows you. You build a connection to what God said and where you are. And because you have clear understanding, you're able to run with the revelation that you've received. Running with the Word means that you've entered a place of flow in God; you've entered into a time and space where you understand clearly that you may be in the world, but you are not of this world; and therefore you cannot be easily fooled, confined, constrained or contained because you know the Word. As an Apostolic and Prophetic people, you simply must know the Word. After all it is the Word that is a light and a lamp unto our feet according to *Psalm 119:105*. The Word not only shows you the way, but it causes the path to be illuminated. In the beginning, the first gift that we received was the Word. Because it is the Word that you must have in order to keep you from being confounded and confined; and apart from it, you can do nothing.

The Word of the Lord states in *John 8:32*, "*you shall know the truth and truth shall make you free.*" The enemy has tried to make many of us believe his lies. If it were at all possible, he would deceive even the elect. This is why it is imperative that you not only know your God, but also the Words that He speaks. In the beginning was the Word and the Word was with God and the Word was God (*John 1:1*). We must not only have the Word, but also apply the Word because the Word does not lie. Your body may be in pain because of sickness and disease, but you have the Word of God and with His stripes you are healed. This does not mean that you will live a trial free life at all. No! I understand that there are some things that are going to manifest, but you must understand that the Word is the Word. It is the Word that will cause you to remain standing on the promises of God. One thing I've learned about our God is that He cannot go against His Word. His Word is truth, it is sharper than any sword, and is a discerner of the thoughts and intent of every heart.

The teacher helps bring to light the Word of God; because, if we receive the word, we can deal with every demon in hell and every adverse situation. You may be wondering how Jesus dealt with the devil. The devil came to Jesus when He was in a place of hunger because He was fasting. The devil tempted him by telling Him to turn those stones into bread. Jesus responded with the Word. If you want to handcuff the enemy, you can do it with the Word of God. He says man shall not live by bread alone but every Word that perceives out of the mouth of God (*Matthew 4:4*). When you open your mouth it is not you, it is the Prophetic utterances of God that will flow out of your mouth like living waters. God wants you to remember that He has placed something inside of you that must be stirred up. That gift is going to come up and out like living waters. Every time the enemy comes with adverse or negative comments and conversations, as an Apostolic and Prophetic people, God has given you the authority, power, and the Word to knock him back to where he came from.

It is the teacher that gives you the Word, but you must apply what has been taught. Many have gotten the word, but simply do not know how to apply it. Application is key, because you have to apply what you have been taught. It cannot just be a Word that lies dormant. We must begin to proactively and deliberately utilize the declared Word as a living part of our daily Kingdom processes. It has to be a Word that you are ready to execute, and it is time that you execute it now. You have to begin to apply that Word. Learn how to make that Word relevant and relate it to your life. The Word will cause you to stand up and say, "I am not going to be stopped, limited, hindered, hemmed up, nor denied any longer because I have the Word of God."

The teacher expounds upon the Word of God that we might be everything that God has called us to be. After digesting the Word and then applying it to our lives, it will begin to challenge the status quo. Everyone will not be able to see what you see, but it is not for them to see, they need to see what it is they need to see so they can be what they see.

If you can see it for you, I can see it for me. The ones that see it can run with it. The one that has an insight about what has been revealed can run with it. The Apostolic and Prophetic are never in conflict. They are not competing; but they are complementary to one another because their goal is to equip the saints and build up the body of Christ. They are here to bring clarity to the vision to illuminate the vision before our mind's eye.

They are working hand in hand, hand in glove. They are moving in the same direction and they want us all to get to the place that God has ordained that we be. There is communion with the Apostle and Prophet because they work together. Then the teacher comes and expounds on what has already been laid. God understood that the people must have a level of the scriptures before they would ever receive the gifts that Christ left. He dealt with the people first; the Apostle, Prophet and then the Teacher before He ever dealt with the gift. If you cannot get the people right, you are not going to experience all of the giftings of God, you have to (get good) with the people.

God wants to remove us from the normal way of doing things. We can no longer remain in a comfortable place, when God is calling and causing us to stretch and expect more. We need one another and must move forward together. In an Apostolic and Prophetic house we must understand that there is more to it than what we see with the naked eye. When we come together we will truly advance the Kingdom of God. The enemy never thought we would get to the place where we are walking as a united front. He never thought we would operate in Kingdom principles on every front. There is work to be done, but there is far more that has been done than what is on our shoulders. It is time to see miracles in the house of God. As Apostles and Prophets, we must prepare the people. They must be positioned properly, before consistent miracles will flow. As we begin to understand the order that is in the house, it will automatically cause a shift. We will then begin to seek God to move in the building. As we seek after Him with all of our being, then we will see Him come into the midst of our situations; and we will see people who have been struggling all of their lives, be delivered. As the Apostle and the Prophet come together, the people will see God like never before in the midst of His assembly as miracles and healing take place and He ushers us into new dimensions.

Apostolic and Prophetic people look for, and operate in miracles, signs and wonders. They believe in the healing power of God because they know that He is able and He desires to see His people be set free. As an Apostolic and Prophetic people, you will move into greater works. You will begin to see the impossible being worked out in your life. Things that once seemed to be obstinate, hard, and stubborn will suddenly become pliable and move out of the believer's way. There are many people who need to be healed naturally. But there are those who need to be spiritually healed because they are wounded and are blind to the things of God. When the healing virtue of God rests on a house, many will begin to operate in the gift that resides in the atmosphere.

James gives specific instructions as he talked about the call of the elders of the Church. The scriptures say that they are to lay hands and anoint with oil so that healing will take place. Eldership has to do with pastoral anointing; when the elders come in they come in meaning business. If there is sickness of any kind, they do not need to come in half stepping or scared, they need to have all of God flowing and operating in and through them. Our God is all that we need; and when you show up, if you show up to do business in the Kingdom, He will honor you. No, this is not the time to take names when God has called you to take over for the Kingdom of God. As you operate in that place, you realize truly that there is a gift on your life. It is not you; it is the gift that He placed on the inside of you. People oftentimes get caught up in the gift(s), when God is trying to get us to understand that we have this treasure in earthen vessels. It is not the gift, it is the Giver; and the Giver for every gift is God. As an Apostle, when I show up I do not show up in my own strength, I show up with the gift of God. I cannot take any credit for the glory that's on my life; it is the gift of God. I am just going to be a vessel and I am yielding myself. However, He wants me to bless people, as His Apostle, that's what I must do.

When people come to an Apostolic and Prophetic house they are looking for direction and help and they must be able to obtain it. Everywhere a believer sits, there should be a person operating in a ministry gift who can help them receive what they need from God. The people should not have to look far to find some help. *Psalm 121* tells us that all of our help comes from the Lord, and that is absolutely true. However, He uses people as conduits of spiritual provision to give you exactly what you need. He can use you to be the answer to that need. He can use you to bring the solution to any problem. God has called us to be the help that is necessary in an atmosphere. I do not know how you feel about it, but if you cannot help me, then I do not want you to hinder me. We need those that are going to help. Husbands need wives that are going to push them; wives need husbands that are going to love them, as Christ loved the Church and gave Himself for her. All of it is help. We are a people that bring help; we are a people that will bring ease; and provoke the people of God to walk in all that God desires.

The Lord gives gifts of healings, helps, and governments. When we speak of Governments, we're speaking of authority; it is the place where you begin to function and your operation deals with laws. As you move into your place in the Apostolic and Prophetic there are laws that God will allow you to be able to maneuver in because the government is upon you; the gift of government that says I know how to operate in authority. I understand how to submit to governmental authority, but at the end of the day I can understand that the government I am functioning under is a much higher government; and therefore, upon His shoulders. Apostolic and Prophetic people understand that although I'm under authority, the authority I am under is functioning under a greater authority which allows me to have more power.

As an Apostle, I must say, if you are not operating in submission under authority then you must know that your authority is not as great as you think that it is. Being under Apostolic order means that you cannot do any and everything you want to do; but you have to understand that there is a divine order, Apostolic governmental order when it comes to the things of the Kingdom. You have to understand that a Prophet is subject to another Prophet; that submission is the way of God, and in the Kingdom things must be done His way. Under Apostolic order, there are diversities (different kinds) of tongues, languages. He is not talking about the unknown tongue, but is speaking of different languages. God gives the gifts of different languages, because He desires that we be able to reach as many as possible for the cause of Christ.

He gave some Apostles, Prophets and evangelists, pastors and some teachers. He set it in order to work together for the perfecting and maturity of the saints. Paul said, when I was a child I spoke as a child; I thought as a child; understood as a child, but when I became a man I put away childish things. Do not allow the enemy to use you. You have to understand when you have matured in God the cycle of who you used to be has to end. No longer can we look for someone to move us emotionally; we should not be attempting to get someone to preach us into oblivion. It is the Lord that matures us to work ministry and He does it through His gifts. He uses the gifts to make us grow enough to deal with childish circumstances. Ministry is work. He gave all the Apostles, Prophets, evangelists, pastors, teachers for the maturing of the saints and the work of the ministry, that we be mature enough to work ministry. In working ministry, I have to deal with sheep that are dirty. I have to get my hands dirty. Some of the people I am feeding do not like me, but I still have to feed them, work with them, and help them get to the place of maturity. If you thought ministry was about skipping through the tulips, you have another thought coming!

We are an Apostolic Church and it's time that we begin to operate totally as one. It is time that we are found functioning and flowing in the fullness of our Apostolic anointing in the Kingdom of God. Everything that pertains to whom He destined us to be requires us to fully function; we certainly don't want to miss Him in this season. As a body, we always want to be on the cutting edge of what God is doing in the earth realm. God is releasing a spirit of precision and power in the earth realm. This is the season that you will not miss God. You are going to have this cutting edge power and Prophetic precision like you have never known before.

Many have been trying to work to get the job done, but I want you to know that the Lord has already completed it. All you have to do is trust Him because He has already completed the work. All you have got to do is walk in what He has completed. He has given you shoes of completion, now it's time to put them on. Understand, however, that once accepted, you will not be able to control them. You will not be able to dictate where they should be going; all you will be able to do is walk in your assignment if you are committed to God's placement and positioning for your life. As Apostolic and Prophetic believers, when you walk in the fullness of what God has called you to, it will free you up. You will begin to notice that you are a whole lot freer than what you have been before. Walking in the fullness means that you will not be confined to people, places or things. It means that you trust Him enough to know that He is leading you, and where He leads, you simply must follow. After all He has already done it and all you are doing is following the footsteps of the path that He created for you to walk in with precision and power.

In this season, I believe that God wants to speak something specifically to His people. To miss the alignment of this hour, will cause you to miss a whole lot more than an hour. God desires for you to walk in everything that He has destined for your life before the foundation of the world. His desire is that you walk in what He has already completed. Did you get that?! It's already a completed work. Once you understand that the work is already completed, then you will begin to walk in the liberty that cannot be removed or taken away from you. God said that He will give us all things (*Romans 8:32*), and He did it already. It's with you! However, He didn't just stop there. He gave some Apostles, those that have a set anointing to lead the way. You see, when you have a true Apostle in your life, there's no way that you can be satisfied being stagnant and stuck wherever you are. It is in this season that God is declaring that if we are going to implement a new order in the Apostolic and Prophetic with the focus of restoring His Church, then no longer can we simply go through the motions. We must no longer be afraid to walk in what Christ has called us to. You and I are ambassadors for God. That means we are sent as representatives for the Kingdom of God. Wherever I go, I am sent as an ambassador. When an ambassador goes to a particular state or area, they are given certain types of immunities. Why is that? We are all serving as official ambassadors. Just as when we go, we are coming in the stead of the King Himself and therefore we are not coming in our own dominion, power, or authority. But we are coming in that of The King, as His Ambassador, who is His representative in the earth. Therefore, we have been given certain authorities because we are serving as He would in that nation or in that kingdom. When you are an ambassador, there are certain rights that are afforded to you, and you have certain privileges. You must understand that as an Apostolic and Prophetic people, when you are serving under the King, He has already given you everything that you need to do His bidding in the earth.

The enemy does not want you to walk in your privileges. He wants you to operate and be contained by the things that you are dealing with in the natural. When you are operating in another realm; another dimension and another world, the places of limitations have been removed. I understand that we can say it in principle, but we must begin to say it in practice. In this season, who we are needs to become our practice. He sent some Apostles. He sent ones that have an anointing to go, and establish the governmental order of God. He sent some Apostles and some Prophets. In *Ephesians 2:12*, the Church is built upon the foundations of the Apostles and the Prophets.

The restoration of the Apostolic Church is transforming the face of the Church from a passive, withdrawn entity into a bold, aggressive, advancing spiritual force - an explosive, expansive, causative force of God. Apostolic people are not passive people. We are not sitting back waiting for things to happen. God has called us to be a people that make things happen according to the Holy Spirit that lives on the inside of us. He has called us to be implements of Kingdom motion and change. Therefore our season of passivity is over. There is no way that we should allow things to just "happen" when the Lord has told us clearly that we can speak those things that be not as though they were. No longer can we stay in the season we are in. The words that come out of our mouths have both light and life. They will either shine and show the way or they will breathe life into our dead dysfunctional situations. As an Apostolic, Prophetic person when I open my mouth I believe God for impossible things to come to pass. We cannot simply sit back and allow a spirit of lethargy or complacency to immobilize us; God expects us to execute what He has already established and ordained. He has already equipped us to move forward, up and out! It is time to challenge our spirit man and make some things happen; it's time to begin to speak the oracles of the Lord. It is God's desire that you began to declare the things of God, so that He can do whatever is good, acceptable and the perfect will of the Father.

When you begin to declare the Word of the Lord, you will truly understand that death and life are in the power of the tongue. God's word will never fall to the ground. *Isaiah 55:11* says that the word of God does not return void, but it will perform what it has been sent to do. You have got to know that when you are operating Apostolically and Prophetically, the winds will carry His word until God performs that word. Your confidence should not be in yourself, but in the power of God.

I believe what God says, and faith really IS the substance of all things hoped for. Faith comes by hearing the word of God. It is the substance of all things hoped for, but the evidence of things not seen. I am hoping for and I have an expectation that what I have spoken will manifest. The Word comes from my belly, proceeds out of my mouth and then it begins to orchestrate and create. When you open your mouth, there should be creative power that is associated with who you are because you belong to God. There is creativity in your words. There are things that are beginning to form just because you open your mouth. You must build confidence in knowing that the words you speak are not your own, they are His Words and He is responsible for bringing them to pass. That is why it is so important that when you pray that you are not praying what you want, but what God says. Speak healing over your body; speak prosperity over your finances, and speak deliverance over those that are lost.

We are in an Apostolic season and you have to begin to declare the change that you want to see. If you do not decree the things that you want to see changed; you'll never see the change. The cycle of the mundane, regular run-of-the-mill kind of Church must be broken. We must break out of that place where we have not seen anything change; where we are not speaking change or expecting change. The Church must rise out of a place of death, awaken from lethargy and receive true revelation regarding the core purpose of the Church. If we look in the book of Acts, they were a bold Church led by Apostles, who partnered with Prophets and teachers. They were not a passive Church; they were busy building the Kingdom of God.

In *1 Corinthians 12*, there is a discussion that we are collectively a part of Christ's Body. Each part specifically and distinctively has its own place and function that God has set in the Church. This distinction is what separates His Church from those that simply desire to go to Church. Because He has given these gifts with specificity, it is the specificity that causes us to understand that God set a divine order in the Kingdom that cannot, and should not be changed by any man-made order that mere humans could ever think of. This new order is not one that we have thought of, but it is an order that is God ordained, placed in the earth, and simply must be God-implemented in order to advance His Kingdom. The gift of the Apostle was left to bring the Body into divine alignment; and to help set order, create strategies, and point the way, so that others may follow. Throughout the Bible, we encounter instances where we see the limitless possibilities of God. I'm so grateful that God does not put limitations on us and the call of the Apostolic anointing. Those limitations came from an enemy that desired to keep the people of God localized; always in the same place, going through the same things, and never walking in the true fullness of all that the Kingdom has to offer. Some may feel that Apostles are not necessary for today or even argue that they are not valid simply because they believe that the only Apostles that existed were those that were named specifically by Christ Himself. However, I beg to differ. Nowhere in scripture will you find it proven or shown that once Jesus finished calling those twelve Apostles, that there were no more to be called. However, what is shown is that Paul's life was marked by religious zeal, violence, and relentless persecution of the early Church. He was never called specifically by Jesus as one of the original twelve, yet he is known by all as one of the greatest Apostles of all time. So, if we are going to follow the order of God, we cannot allow anyone to put limitations on us, we cannot even put them on ourselves. We simply must be a people that will read it and believe that it is so, even for us today. The word of God must be taken in context because the Divine Order of God cannot be limited by your ingenuity or your genius. The genius of God is that He does not rely on our intellect to prove who He is. He is God whether we believe Him to be or not. He is God and God all by Himself. He does not need our approval to be God. He does not need our pat on the back to be God. He just is. As God was sending Moses, He told Him to reply to the people as they asked who sent him: "I Am has sent me," As "Sent Ones" this should always be our response when someone questions your call, and the answer should be the same...."I AM has sent me." There is no need for competition in the Body. What sense does it make for the baby toe to compete with the big toe, or the elbow to compete with the thumb? They each have their own specific area of operation just as each body part in Christ. When we are representing the I Am, there should be neither competition nor comparison and neither does God need your approval to be who He is and neither should you if you are in God. He said that He appointed these in the Church - first Apostles. One of the things about the Apostle is that they set governmental order. Governmental order means that there is a way that God operates. It is the way God moves, and when, how, and where He moves. As His people, we ought to be moving just like that!

Conclusion
Ephesians 2:20-22

Ephesians 4:11-12, reminds us that "he gave some Apostles; and some Prophets; some, evangelists; and some, pastors and teachers; For the perfecting of the saints, for the work of the ministry, for the edifying of the body of Christ: Till we all come in the unity of the faith, and of the knowledge of the Son of God, unto a perfect man, unto the measure of the stature of the fullness of Christ." As Apostles and Prophets, God has sanctioned us to work together to implement this New Order in restoring His Church back to His original plan. God desires for His Body to mature and grow and not be stagnated and stuck, but ever evolving into the perfect man. One thing I know for certain is that though the foundation is built on the Apostle and the Prophet, there is room for everyone! Therefore, whatever your gift, talent, or calling is, if ever you were going to pursue Him, now is the time to do it with all of your might. As a matter of fact, take the limits off and do it with reckless abandon! I submit to you that it's time that we all find our place in advancing the Kingdom and perfect that place by committing to prayer, studying His Word, and then by doing the work of the ministry. It is then that we will truly see *A New Order of Apostolic and Prophetic Restoration of His Church.*

It is the Word of the Lord concerning you!
All the glory belongs to Almighty God!

www.ingramcontent.com/pod-product-compliance
Lightning Source LLC
Chambersburg PA
CBHW060432050426
42449CB00009B/2249